Houston Unleashed

Text by John DeMers

Story by Rhonda K. Findley

Photographs by E. Joseph Deering

Unleashed Books

Houston • New Orleans

For additional copies, send $9.95 plus $2.00 S&H to:
Unleashed Books / P.O. Box 610034 / Houston, TX 77208-0034

ACKNOWLEDGEMENTS

First and foremost, we want to thank two special Houstonians for letting Indy borrow their beloved pets for days spent "unleashed": Donna and Richard Carson for Patch (who portrays Sam in the story) and Judy Nichols for Star (who appears as the lovely Doreen). As you'd guess, we'd never have been able to get these pictures without plenty of generous help, in this case coming from all the sites pictured in these pages. Special thanks go to: Hobby Airport, the Reliant Astrodome, Six Flags Astro World/Water World, Space Center, Kemah Boardwalk, San Jacinto State Historical Park, Enron Field, the Museum of Fine Arts Houston, the Children's Museum, Michael Kemper Salon and Day Spa, Central Market, Tiffany at the Galleria, and of course, tony's and its master, Tony Vallone. Additional thanks are due: Dancie Perugini Ware and her staff, John Dickinson, Dick Dace, Sandra Lawson, Melissa Burkhart, Vanessa Brown, Jeff Louviere, Alison Wells, and everyone at the Houston Chronicle.

With my family – my parents, my boy and my girl –
I landed in Houston, all Hobby aswirl.
Though they might have been dog food, I'd played a big hunch,
Rejecting the peanuts they'd served me for lunch.

At our trip's first stop,
    my stomach got serious:
If I didn't go somewhere,
    I might go delirious.
So between thoughts of feasting
    and longings for home,
I slipped unnoticed
    from the Astrodome.

Don't get me wrong,
I had no plan,
No sense of Houston,
where it stopped or began.

It seemed one big freeway, buzzing lane after lane.
Filled with drivers who blended inept with insane.

Remembering my young ones, wishing they were around,
I wistfully followed my ears toward the sound.
Six Flags was the kind of place they'd adore,
Racing for hours and begging for more.

I spent a wild hour surviving the rides,

Being tipped and tustled and tosse...

When the last coaster settled, solid ground got a kiss –
To think my family would pay money for this!

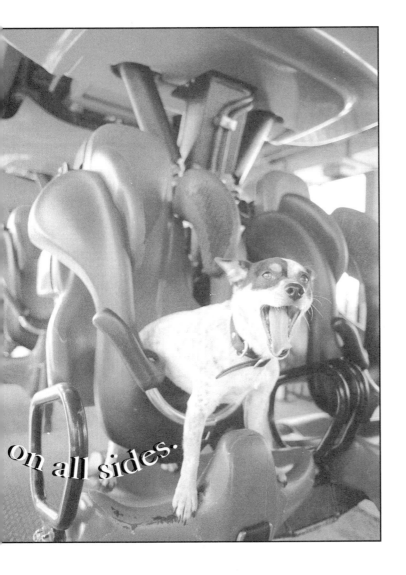

on all sides.

9

By this time, the sun
beat down in midday,
The kind that in Houston
takes your breath away.
I grabbed a few turns
past a big guard's scowl,
And chilled like a lifeguard
without swimsuit or towel.

Water World shimmers
in the hot Texas sun,
To toss you in wave pool,
to shoot you from gun.
I barked my last words
on the slide, like a rube,
But I lived to be lazy —
one cool pup in a tube.

I hitched a quick ride
    on a truck into space,
Or at least to the place
    that won the moon race.
Space Center showed me
    bright things that go up,
Though no one said, "Houston,
    we have a pup."

Mission Control
    was intriguing to me.
It made me hope
    to someday see
My own pawprints
    in moondust signed:

"One small step for a dog, one giant leap for Dogkind."

At a place called Kemah, the waterfront
Serves up any seafood you could ever want,
From dancing fountain to carousel refrain -
If you get tired of boardwalk, you can just jump the train.

While I was out wandering,
I toured San Jacinto,
The park with the Lone Star
monu-memento.

Here Texas won freedom
for Star, Patch and Rover,
With a ship to protect it
over and over.

19

As soon as Texas said,
     "Adios, Santa Anna,"
The place went Republic,
     with one top banana.
Sam Houston loomed large
     as two guys formed a city,
So they named it for Sam,
     and not just for pretty.

Allen and Kirby
saw a buck to be made
With cotton and rice
they'd have it made in the shade
Come live in paradise
crowed their real estate pitch -
When they had but a bayou
just an overgrown ditch

On this day, that real estate was afternoon blue.
It promised adventure, or at least things to do.
With no final look, my sad eyes turned down,
I grabbed a stuttering Metro downtown.

The ride was rough, the detours many,
The bus hunted potholes, and didn't miss any.
The traffic clogged, so I stopped for a swim.
If I meet Mr. Mecom, I'll have to thank him.

23

Back on the street in the heart of it all,
Downtown was a mix of palace and stall.
From dust and spill and spoil it rose,
spewing lofts with big windows
                    to show off great clothes.

I'd pictured cowboys
in ten-gallon tops
And two-stepping honky tonks
that pulled out all stops.
I'd pictured oil derricks
gushing out black gold –
My vision of Houston
was just a wee bit old.

25

Aware of my starving, I trolled between feet,
Seeking calzone, burritos, even sushi to eat.
The pickings were slim, the leavings not much –
My paws padded pavement that cooked at first touch.

"Hey buddy," a voice graveled
   from an alley behind.
"If you're lookin' for lunch here,
   then you gotta be blind.
Can't you see high-class handouts
   will always be lame –
To take in some real food, man,
   take in a game!"

Enron's the place.
    He said there's no better
For chow and a drink
    and a 'Stros double-header.
The place is alive
    with hits, runs and outs –
Not to mention big burgers,
    without any sprouts.

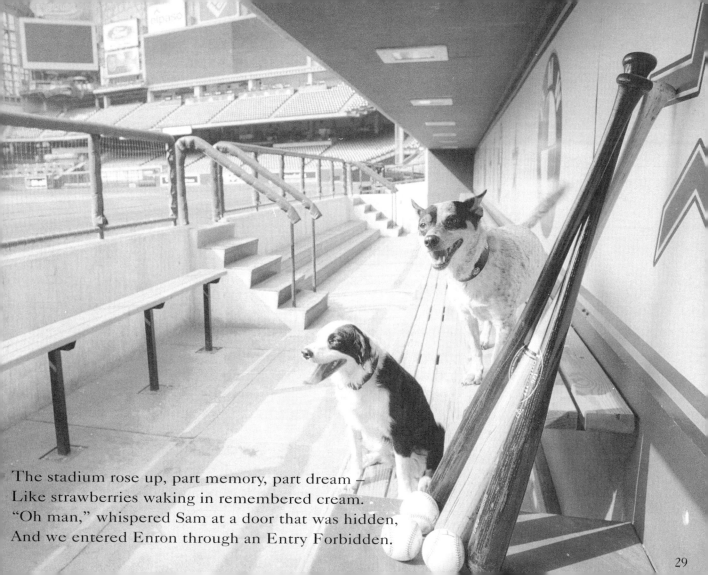

The stadium rose up, part memory, part dream —
Like strawberries waking in remembered cream.
"Oh man," whispered Sam at a door that was hidden,
And we entered Enron through an Entry Forbidden.

29

The kitchen was bursting
with nacho and wing -
Foodservice for thousand
is a marvelous thing
We feasted unseen
then we feasted some more
With no glimpse of game
and no thought of score

We ate our way onward, up food chain and down,
Till I thought they'd have to roll me from town.
And when our banquet at last reached its end –

A soft voice said, "Hi Sam. Who *is* your cute friend?"

"A new dog in town," our Sam told Doreen,
(Who may be the best-looking pup ever seen).
"But show him some mercy, he's not for you;
You like them lots older, and lots richer too!"

I felt shy and awkward,
decidedly fat,
As her eyes drifted over me
this way and that.
Her smile curled upward,
all delight or deception.
"For him," she told Sam,
"I'll make an exception."

So it was written.
And it came to pass,
That I left Enron Field
with my classy new lass.
"Don't mind me,
oh don't worry at all,"
Mumbled Sam as he set off
in search of baseball.

"I'm Indy," I told her.
"You should know my name."
And we touched paws in greeting,
strolling out of the game.
She led me past bayous,
in sunlight, through breeze,
Till we reached something
I hadn't seen in a while – trees.

The parks were lovely,
the fountains cool,
Making mirrors for passage
in pool after pool.
We checked out
the old masters at MFA,
Then sipped on a latte
in a Montrose café.

The Children's Museum
offered smaller delights,
Teaching ups and downs
and wrongs and rights.
The kids in these halls
got to be a bit much.
But for once the signs
on the wall said

"Please Touch!"

39

Our walk out Westheimer
    was wild with surprise,
With trinkets and treasures
    intriguing our eyes.

As for funk, punk and hippie, we saw all that too—
Thank goodness I got out without a tattoo!

40

TATTOOS
DONE
DAILY

We strolled without rushing,
    singing songs, telling jokes
Showing off for her boyfriends
    in green River Oaks.
We wrote our own poem,
    she taught me to bark it

In the blocks out to Michael's
and Central Market.

In the dusk things got dicey,
all traffic and noise,
As children played chicken
in four-wheeled toys.
We raced beneath roadways
with sprint, spring and stoop.
"You are now," Doreen told me,
"Outside the Loop."

It's different, she said, with a wave of her hand,
Stretching miles to Spring, Katy and Sugar Land.
As for me, smiled Doreen, I need an epiphany,
The kind that's delivered by Neiman or Tiffany.

It's a girl thing, I thought,
since ages Jurasstic,
Whether swapping for seashells
or plunking down plastic.
Through store after store,
with giggling and stopping,
The truth is: I never had
so much fun shopping.

48

We ran out of hours,
　　Galleria Time,
Which works out way less
　　than a second per dime.
She filled bags with perfumes
　　and porcelain ponies –
Just the stuff to drag in
　　for dinner at tony's.

The wait staff angled to accommodate,
Since Doreen was a regular, both early and late.
They piled her bounty behind a dark wooden door –
They'd clearly seen conspicuous consumption before.

And then something happened
    to unravel my ruffle,
Between pasta with lobster
    and hen with black truffle.
Our waiter drew back,
    as though onto a shelf,
To make way for our moment
    with Tony himself.

"Excuse me," he said,
    bending over our table,
"But you need to know something
    as soon as you're able.
If this dog is Indy –
    and I'm certain you are –
Thanks to Houston TV,
    you're a bit of a star!"

My family was televised,
in clips long and short,
Showing my picture
in every report.
It was simple,
I suddenly understood from above:
There are limits to patience,

but never to love.

This way, someone said,
the Mayor's sending a car
To get where you're going
from here where you are.
This is cause for great joy,
no reason for sorrow –
I'll bet you're Page One
in The Chronicle tomorrow.

My date and I snuggled on that drive through the night,
Back to my family, to make each wrong right.
Though touched and teary, she was *still* my Doreen,
At home with her shopping –

in a stretch limousine!

INDY'S FAVORITES

Hobby Airport: One of two major airline hubs in Houston, Hobby handles a busy schedule of regional flights each day. Many travelers are drawn to Hobby by its close-in location and ease of access to downtown and most other commercial sections of the metropolitan area. Houston's other airport, George Bush Intercontinental, handles domestic flights too, plus a broad array of connections to capitals in Europe, Latin America and far beyond.

Reliant Astrodome: The world's first domed stadium (1965) was long the home to the city's sports teams, including of course the Houston Astros. Now it's part of a larger sports and exhibition complex carrying the name Reliant Energy. The complex features a new football stadium for the new NFL franchise, the Houston Texans. Many locals take a nostalgic "tour" of the Astrodome each February, when the Houston Livestock Show and Rodeo is held there, featuring all the usual lifestock plus big-name musical entertainment.

Six Flags Astro World/Water World: Stretching out on the far side of the 610 Loop from the new Reliant complex, these twin thrill parks offer fun and excitement for children and adults alike. At Six Flags, grownups can opt for the Texas Tornado, the world's steepest four-loop coaster, while little ones prefer Looney Tunes Town. Water World offers a kaleidescope of water slides and other splash-filled summer attractions.

Space Center Houston: Modern history meets family fun in this collection of memories from America's space adventure. Highlights include real Mercury, Gemini and Apollo capsules, plus Texas' largest IMAX theater and tours of the famed Johnson Space Center. There's lots of hands-on, space-theme excitement for the young astronaut-to-be.

Kemah Boardwalk: Though the fishing village of Kemah has been around a long time, it has only been transformed into a dining and entertainment destination in the past few years. The dusty old (if colorful) seafood houses have been replaced by Landry's, Joe's Crab Shack and all their corporate kin, including a newer place themed around an aquarium full of exotic fish. A Ferris wheel, a train, arcade games and more fill out the fun.

San Jacinto State Historical Park: This is the 1,000-acre site east of Houston where Texas won its independence in 1836, when Sam Houston led 820 Texans to victory over the Mexican forces commanded by Gen. Santa Anna. There is a dramatic obelisk that's actually taller than the Washington Monument, plus the grand old Battleship Texas – the only surviving Navy warship that served in both World Wars.

Enron Field: Part of Houston's downtown renaissance, Enron is home to the National League's Houston Astros. After years of playing in the Astrodome, the team now enjoys Enron's retractable roof, a nifty piece of engineering that brings traditional outdoor baseball to Houston. Other days at the height of Texas summer, the air conditioning under the roof feels mighty good.

Museum District: Houston is home to more than 500 cultural, visual and performing arts organizations. This district gathered around Hermann Park and the familiar Mecom Fountain features, among many attractions, the Museum of Fine Arts and its Audrey Beck Building, the oh-so-hands-on Children's Museum, the Houston Museum of Natural Science (with its own IMAX and the six-story Cockrell Butterfly Center), the Contemporary Arts Museum and the eclectic Menil Collection.

Westheimer: One of the longest and most diverse roadways you'll encounter anywhere, Westheimer features everything from quirky used-clothing shops and ramshackle tattoo parlors to hyper-chic restaurants and hair salons, such as the day spa operated by famed stylist Michael Kemper. New to

Westheimer is Central Market, a Texas-born food-as-entertainment complex that seems certain to change the way you think about groceries.

Galleria Area: Years before every city on the planet had one or more shopping malls, Houston had the Galleria. It remains consumerism's crown jewel, for its restaurants, its ice skating rink and its collection of top-line stores such as Neiman Marcus, Fendi, Gucci, Armani and Tiffany. Locals love to finish off their days of Galleria shopping with dinner nearby at tony's, the flagship restaurant founded by Tony Vallone.

ABOUT THE HUMANS

John DeMers, a native of New Orleans, is the new food editor of the Houston Chronicle, having followed Ann Criswell's 34 years in that position. He is the author of 23 previous books and has written about food, wine and travel from more than 120 foreign countries. He has also scripted five produced, one-person dramas and starred in two of them.

Little Rock native Rhonda Findley lives in the historic Marigny neighborhood of New Orleans, where she writes about food and wine, cohosts a weekly radio show on those subjects called Delicious Mischief, and is the co-author of New Orleans Unleashed. She also takes care of Indy, star of both Houston and New Orleans Unleashed, and his rescued brother Presston.

Photographer E. Joseph Deering was born in Michigan and trained at the prestigious Brooks Institute in Santa Barbara, Calif. He has spent the past three decades as a staff photographer for the Houston Chronicle.